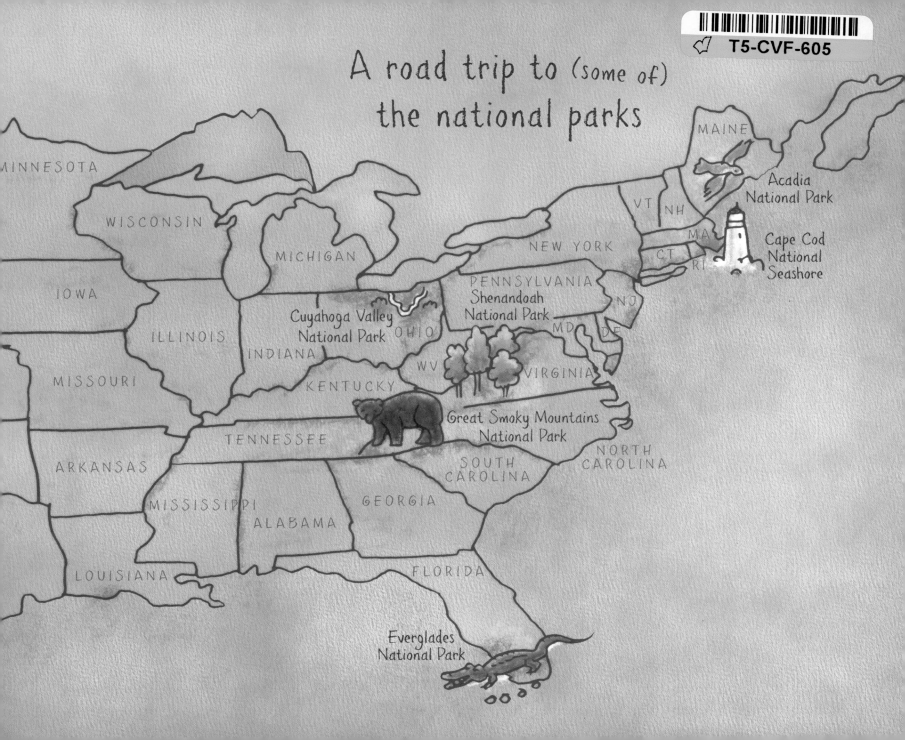

A road trip to (some of) the national parks

Time for National Parks

Written by Deanna Neil

Illustrated by Tom Newsom

the ecoseekers™

the ecoseekers

Published by The EcoSeekers™
Copyright © 2010 by Little Green Dreams, LLC
d/b/a The EcoSeekers™

Conceived and produced by David Neil   Text by Deanna Neil
Interior illustrations by Tom Newsom
Scrapbook and endpaper map illustrations by Chris Vallo
Art direction and book design by Paula Winicur

Designed in the United States of America. Printed in Canada.
10 9 8 7 6 5 4 3 2 1

This book is printed on Forest Stewardship Council-certified paper, using soy-based ink.

Mixed Sources
Cert no. SW-COC-001271
© 1996 FSC

The EcoSeekers™ is a proud member of the Green Press Initiative.

green press INITIATIVE

PHOTO CREDITS
My Travel Journal Introduction Courtesy of the National Park Service
Acadia TOP: Courtesy of the National Park Service; SLUG AND STARFISH: Public domain stock
Cape Cod National Seashore Courtesy of the National Park Service
Everglades National Park Courtesy of the U.S. Geological Survey
Cuyahoga Valley National Park Courtesy of William J. Dragga
Shenandoah National Park Courtesy of the National Park Service
Great Smoky Mountains National Park Public domain
Badlands National Park LEFT: Courtesy of J. Crocker; RIGHT: Public domain
Glacier National Park Courtesy of the U.S. Fish and Wildlife Services
Grand Teton National Park Courtesy of the U.S. Fish and Wildlife Service
Rocky Mountain National Park LEFT: Courtesy of the National Park Service; RIGHT: Courtesy of L. VanSickle
Arches National Park Courtesy of the National Park Service
Bryce Canyon National Park Courtesy of the U.S. Fish and Wildlife Services
Grand Canyon National Park Courtesy of the National Park Service
Joshua Tree National Park Public domain
Sequoia and Kings Canyon National Parks TREES: Courtesy of the National Park Service; CHARLES YOUNG: Courtesy of the U.S. Army
Yosemite National Park Courtesy of the National Park Service
Mount Rainier National Park LEFT: Courtesy of the National Park Service; UPPER RIGHT: Public domain
Olympic National Park Courtesy of the National Park Service

Deanna Neil is an eight-time award winning children's book author, named a "Hero of the Planet" by Time Magazine for Kids.

Tom Newsom graduated from Art Center College Of Design, and has since worked as a children's book illustrator, along with his wife and fellow artist, Carol. They live in the foothills of Colorado, surrounded by the inspiring beauty of the Rocky Mountains.

ISBN 978-0-9798800-6-3

— My travel journal —
the national parks

It's time for parks.
There's much to do!
Wake up, put on your
hiking shoes.

Time for seashores,
shells, and sands,
and morning mists on distant lands.

Time together
by a lush creekside.
There's trails to hike
and bikes to ride!

Time for mangroves
and marshy swamps.
(Look out for crocodile
and alligator romps!)

Explore mountain forests,
track deer and moles.
Find secret meadows
with burrowing voles.

Time for fishing and foggy ground. (Busy mosquitoes are buzzing around!)

Time for moose
and big black bears,
for burly bison
and hopping hares.

Time for minnows and hungry beaks,
for jutting cliffs with snowy peaks.

Time for deserts,
sun-baked buttes,
fallen antlers and cactus fruits.

Time for camping and granola bars. Time for sleeping under stars.

Put out your fire,
eat your last s'more,
crawl into your tent on
a pine-covered floor.

Follow the rivers,
dance with the streams.
It's time for nature,
time for dreams.

It's time.
It's time.
The adventure is yours and mine.

— My travel journal —
the national parks

Acadia National Park

Cape Cod National Seashore

Everglades National Park

Cuyahoga Valley National Park

Shenandoah National Park

Great Smoky Mountains National Park

Badlands National Park

Glacier National Park

Yellowstone National Park

Grand Teton National Park

Rocky Mountain National Park

Arches National Park

Bryce Canyon National Park

Zion National Park

Grand Canyon National Park

Joshua Tree National Park

Sequoia and Kings Canyon National Parks

Redwood National Park

Yosemite National Park

Mount Rainier National Park

Olympic National Park

↑ Shenandoah National Park

↑ Glacier National Park

← Bryce Canyon National Park

↓ Olympic National Park

Grand Teton National Park ↓

Acadia National Park (est. 1917)

America's first national park on the east coast.

Climbed part of Cadillac Mountain, the <u>tallest</u> mountain on the U.S. Atlantic Coast — 1,530 feet!

GEORGE B. DORR

(1855–1944)

George B. Dorr is known as the father of Acadia National Park. He spent his own money and much of his life creating and expanding the park to protect nature for the public to enjoy.

Eeewww!
Found these **slugs** on mushrooms. There are lakes and forests here, too. The ocean was too cold so we swam in Echo Lake.

Sea star found in a tidepool.

There are lots of old shipwrecks.

Cape Cod National Seashore

est. 1961

This is a national seashore, not a park.

The original Highland Lighthouse was built in 1797. It was the first lighthouse on Cape Cod. There are lots of archeological sites. Humans have been on Cape Cod for 9,000 years.

It's also a peninsula, which means the land pokes out into the Atlantic Ocean.

The beaches here are awesome. Lots of crabs live on the beach. We saw a HUUUUGE one!

We saw a little baby turtle. They are not endangered but there are fewer and fewer of them. Cape Cod National Seashore supports 32 species that are rare or endangered in Massachusetts.

Everglades National Park

est. 1947

We were prepared for mosquito bites, but there were tons of bugs.

Got one!

Toads and frogs were singing all day like a choir. There are over 50 kinds of reptiles here. But I'm keeping my eye out for this one.

Everglades

Welcome to the Everglades! The Everglades is the largest subtropical wilderness in the United States.

Everglades National Park is the only place where the Amercian crocodile and alligator coexist.

The Morning Glory, a native species

Cuyahoga Valley National Park

The Cuyahoga River is 100 miles long and flows north to south through the valley.

est. 2000

A Native American word that means "Crooked River"

This place is very green and forested. Beavers and all kinds of birds live here. One special bird is the great blue heron.

The river used to be so nasty and polluted that it once caught fire! It was cleaned up, and now there's lots of wildlife again, but we still can't swim in it.

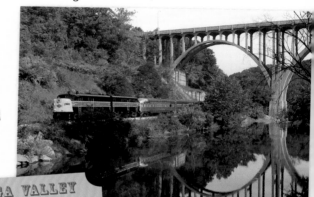

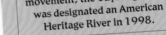

CUYAHOGA VALLEY

For its role in the environmental movement, the Cuyahoga River was designated an American Heritage River in 1998.

SCENIC RAILROAD

Like other tourists, I rode the Cuyahoga Valley Scenic Railroad, which goes more than 20 miles through the park. We saw the remains of the old Ohio and Erie Canal. The first steam engine here went down the new Valley Railway in 1880. This picture shows what the trains look like now.

Shenandoah National Park   est. 1935

Just 75 miles from Washington, D.C., America's capital.

Rapidan Camp, the nation's first "summer White House," was built by President Herbert Hoover in 1929. Hoover built this retreat near a trout stream so he could go fishing.

There are lots of oak and hickory trees all along the Appalachian Trail. Lots of deer chomping away, too. And I saw a woodpecker!

Blue Ridge Mountains

Great Smoky Mountains National Park

est. 1934

America's most visited national park!

This is the "Salamander Capital of the World." I saw 3 red ones, and one that was black and yellow. The Smokies have the most biological diversity of any area in the world's temperate zone.

Great Smoky Mountains National Park was created after thousands of acres of private land were bought and donated to the government with money raised by many people — even school children pledged their pennies.

Kids helped create the park!

Temperate zone
The part of the globe between the tropics and the polar circles with milder temperatures.

Badlands National Park

est. 1978

Cool word. It means "lots of eroded lands with little plant life." Petrified Forest National Park in Arizona is also a "badlands".

This is what a fossil looks like. I found these on the Fossil Exhibit Trail and the Cliff Shelf Nature Trail.
  The Badlands have the world's richest fossil beds from 28-37 million years ago, when the first primates were around.

Geology = study of rocks
Erosion = when something like a rock is worn or washed away over time

Glacier National Park

 est. 1910

The world's 10th national park.
Over 700 miles of trails!

I used my binoculars
and saw this mountain
goat. He looked old
and wise. I felt like all
the wolves, cougars,
lynx, wolverines, bighorn
sheep, elk, moose, and
grizzly bears were also
watching me!

This swinging bridge was scary. We hiked the
South Shore Two Medicine Trail and then
dangled our legs over the creek.

Most scientists believe that global warming will cause the park's
glaciers to melt away soon. That would be weird — no glaciers
in a place called "Glacier" National Park!

ACTIVE
VOLCANO
ALERT!!!

Yellowstone National Park

est. 1872

The world's first national park! The park is mostly in
Wyoming, but also extends into Montana and Idaho.

Old Faithful Geyser. There are
more than 10,000 hot springs in
Yellowstone — that's half the hot
springs in the whole world.

Buffalo roam free in the park.
One came right up to our car window
and its head was huge.

Grand Teton National Park

est. 1929

John D. Rockefeller helped establish this park.

We hiked around String Lake.

Grand Teton 13,770 feet

Middle Teton 12,804 feet

Mount Owen 12,928 feet

South Teton 12,514 feet

Teewinot 12,325 feet

WYOMING

Rocky Mountain National Park, Yellowstone National Park, and Grand Teton National Park are all on the Rocky Mountain Range, which is super long. The mountains go from Canada all the way to New Mexico.

Rocky Mountain National Park

est. 1915

We drove on Trail Ridge Road, high above the tree line across the alpine tundra. Amazing views! Saw elk and bighorn sheep, and lots of wildflowers, too!

We did lots of hiking. My favorite was Bear Lake! There are 359 miles of trails in the park. Some people even hike up Longs Peak at 14,259 feet!

Arches National Park

est. 1971

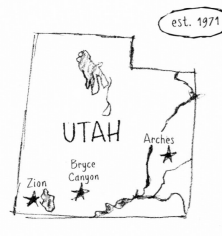

UTAH

Arches

Bryce Canyon

Zion

This is called Delicate Arch. It's the most famous, but there are over 2,000 natural sandstone arches here. Humans have lived here since the last Ice Age, 10,000 years ago.

There are lots of lizards here in the desert. One ran across my foot when we were hiking.

We met with a ranger who taught us about the night sky and astronomy. Our universe is called the Milky Way.

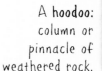

Bryce Canyon National Park

est. 1924

Named after Ebenezer Bryce, a pioneer who homesteaded here.

A **hoodoo**: column or pinnacle of weathered rock.

Zion National Park

Utah's first national park.

est. 1919

This place looks like giant sand castles with canyons. We drove through tunnels carved into the mountains, and hiked at Angels Landing.

Most animals hide out here during the day because it's so hot. The ranger said there are snakes and tarantulas here. Eeek! Supposedly they're nice, but I'm glad I didn't see any.

290 different types of birds fly through Zion every year. By 1970, the peregrine falcon was almost extinct, mostly because of pollution. After people learned more about pesticides and other problems, laws were passed to protect birds. Now there are thousands of falcons.

Grand Canyon National Park est. 1919

This is a World Heritage Site,
and one of the seven natural wonders of the world!

I did a ranger program with the National
Park Service and learned more
about geology, like that the river
helped carve out the canyon.
We also saw the Tusayan Ruins
and learned that Ancestral
Puebloans were the first farmers
about 800 years ago. This place
was their home, and it was sacred.
The Hopi are their descendents.

GRAND
CANYON
Junior
Ranger

The canyon was
wider than anything
I've ever seen. We
went to Mather
Point on the South
Entrance Road,
where most people
visit, and we hiked
down the Bright Angel Trail.
Grandma and Grandpa went on
a mule ride to the Colorado River,
but I'm too short. You have to be
at least 4 feet 7 inches to go.

Joshua Tree National Park

This place was almost named Desert Plants
National Park because of its plant diversity. est. 1994

We saw a desert bighorn herd!

The California deserts have more
than a dozen species of bats —
Earth's only flying mammal.

We watched some crazy rock
climbers. Joshua Tree has more
than 400 climbing formations and
8,000 climbing routes.

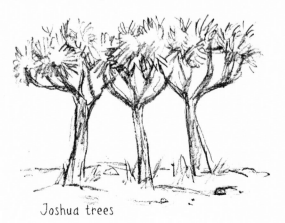

Joshua trees

Sequoia and Kings Canyon National Parks

Together, these parks protect 265 Native American archeological sites and 69 historic sites.

est. 1890

The rings tell you the story of the tree.

This is a scar that shows fire damage.

These trees are enormous! And they are between 600 and 3,000 years old! They get big because they grow fast over a long lifetime. They aren't taken over by many bugs or diseases, and they can survive most fires. The "General Sherman Tree," a sequoia tree in the park, is the largest living tree in the world!

CHARLES YOUNG

Charles Young became the first African-American superintendent of a national park in 1903. He brought his all-black military company from San Francisco to Sequoia to build roads, which brought visitors to the mountaintop forest for the first time.

Redwood National Park

est. 1968

Home of the world's tallest trees! The coastal redwood trees can grow over 300 feet tall. The sequoia trees here are not as wide around as those found in Sequoia and Kings Canyon National Park, but they are taller. Redwood National and State Parks protect almost half of the remaining old redwood trees in California. Redwood trees are also protected in Muir Woods National Monument.

Yosemite National Park

est. 1890

Designated a World Heritage Site in 1984. The Mariposa Grove also has giant sequoias.

Merced River

John Muir was an environmentalist who helped create Yosemite.

Bridalveil falls. There are tons of waterfalls here. It's awesome!

Mount Rainier National Park

(est. 1899) America's 5th national park!

We hiked the Nisqually Vista Trail in Paradise Area and got to see cool views of Mount Rainier and the Nisqually Glacier. Also walked under big douglas fir and hemlock trees. There were some hot springs, too, with bubbling water.

Mount Rainier has the largest glacial system in the contiguous 48 states, consisting of 26 major glaciers covering 335 square miles.

Carbon Glacier, on the north side of Mt. Rainier, comes to the lowest elevation of any glacier in the lower 48 states at 3,500 feet. It is also Mt. Rainier's thickest glacier, one section being nearly 700 feet thick.

(est. 1938) # Olympic National Park

Part of the park is actually a rainforest. That explains why there is so much rain!

Whales, dolphins, sea lions, seals, and sea otters feed in the Pacific Ocean. Olympic has some animals that can't be found anywhere else in the world: Olympic marmots, Olympic snow moles, and Olympic torrent salamanders.

ROOSEVELT ELK

Almost named "Elk National Park", Olympic was primarily created in order to protect these noble creatures from overhunting. It is now home to the largest unmangaged herd of Roosevelt Elk in the world.

Can't wait to add more parks to my journal next year...

HELP PROTECT OUR NATIONAL PARKS

These photos show how air pollution affects visibility within Great Smoky Mountains National Park. On a clear day, views can extend over 100 miles.

polluted day

clear day

Learn more. Get involved.

Help protect our natural treasures for future generations.

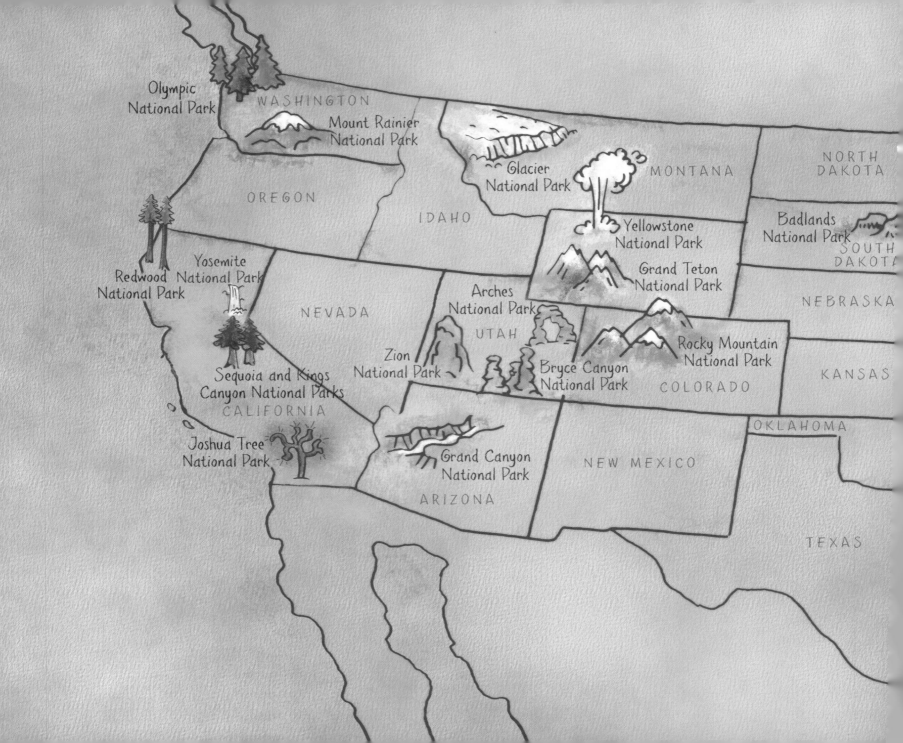